Dorset's Lost Railway

by
Peter Dale

An 0-4-4T at Spetisbury Station in Joint Railway days. The disc and crossbar pattern signal survived until about 1900.

© Peter Dale, 2001
First published in the United Kingdom, 2001,
reprinted 2012
by Stenlake Publishing Ltd,
01290 551122
www.stenlake.co.uk

ISBN 9781840336054

ACKNOWLEDGEMENTS
I would like to thank my father for introducing me to this absorbing hobby and Ken Jones for introducing me to this project.

The publishers wish to thank the following for contributing pictures to this book: John Alsop for the front cover, inside front cover, pages 1–11, 14, 16–31, 33–48, inside back cover, and the back cover; Neville Stead and B.G. Tweed for page 12; and W.A.C. Smith for pages 13, 15 and 32.

A 57xx class pannier tank engine at Bridport Shed, August 1947.

INTRODUCTION

Dorset is a county of thatched cottages, a place for holidays by the sea, and it is Hardy country. Weymouth remains a holiday destination and the nearby naval base at Portland was once of great importance.

The earliest railways in the county were connected with the clay industry on the Isle of Purbeck. The Middlebere Plateway was built in 1806 and linked the clay pits near Norden with a wharf on Middlebere Creek. It was horse-worked and used 3 feet long plates, set on stone sleepers, rather than edge rails. It seems to have remained in use until the early twentieth century.

Early public railways in the county were conceived as parts of plans for links with Exeter by both the London & South Western Railway (LSWR), to compete with the Great Western Railway (GWR), and by the GWR to provide a more direct route than its circuitous great way round through Bristol. Geographically this created difficulties as rivers and valleys in the county tend to be north to south while the desired direction for railways was east to west. In the event, the LSWR main line to Exeter ran mainly just north of Dorset, while the GWR direct line to the west did not touch Dorset at all. The LSWR lines were standard gauge (4 feet 8½ inches and sometimes referred to as narrow gauge) while the GWR lines were built to the broad gauge of 7 feet.

Many of the railways were proposed and built by local companies which were often backed by one of the larger companies. The processes of amalgamation and absorption led to the county being dominated by the GWR and the LSWR which, in terms of route mileage, were respectively the largest and eighth largest of the pre-grouping companies. In 1923, when the railway companies were grouped into the 'Big Four', the LSWR became part of the Southern, although the GWR kept its identity, having absorbed a number of smaller companies. There was, however, another major company involved in Dorset – the Somerset & Dorset Joint Railway, which was known as the 'Slow and Dirty' to its detractors and the 'Swift and Delightful' to its admirers. At the time of the grouping this railway was jointly owned by the Midland Railway and the LSWR and, as the Midland became part of the London, Midland & Scottish Railway (LMS) in 1923, the Somerset & Dorset retained some distinctive features. All of these companies were nationalised as British Railways in 1948.

An engine crew at Weymouth. The locomotive is an 0-6-0T, no. 1376, which was originally built as no. 114 by the Bristol & Exeter Railway for the Culm Valley line in Devon.

Southampton & Dorchester Railway *

Passenger service withdrawn	4 May 1964
Distance	60.5 miles
Company	Southampton & Dorchester Railway

Stations closed	*Date*
Ashley Heath Halt	4 May 1964

Stations closed	*Date*
West Moors for Ferndown	4 May 1964
Wimborne	4 May 1964
Broadstone **	7 March 1966
Creekmoor Halt (Branksome curve)	7 March 1966

West Moors Station. This station was also the junction for the line to Salisbury.

RAILWAY STATION. WEST MOORS.

R.B. BROWN

* The closed stations on this line in Hampshire were Holmsley and Ringwood.

** Also known as Broadstone Junction, Broadstone and New Poole Junction, Poole Junction, Poole Junction and Broadstone and Broadstone (Dorset), to differentiate it from Broadstone, on the Weston, Clevedon & Portishead Railway in Somerset.

Broadstone was an important junction with lines to the north, to the Somerset & Dorset Railway, and to Salisbury and Brockenhurst. To the south lines led to Poole and Bournemouth and Hamworthy Junction.

This line came about largely due to the efforts of a Mr Castleman, a solicitor from Wimborne, and because of its twisting nature it was known as 'Castleman's Corkscrew'. It opened in June 1847 and was absorbed by the LSWR the following year. It was one of no less than four schemes for a direct route to Exeter, two of each gauge, in the late 1840s and in 1852 the LSWR guaranteed a double track coastal route, only having to back down when a meeting of shareholders would not support it, leading to an upheaval on the Board. Exeter finally got its direct standard gauge route, but to the north, via Yeovil, and Dorchester would never be part of a major east–west route. The Southampton & Dorchester had running powers from Dorchester to Weymouth and began running over this section when the GWR route to Weymouth opened in 1857. When the line opened Bournemouth was no more than a hamlet but grew rapidly and to improve rail links with it the Branksome curve and the Holes Bay curve opened in June 1893. After this the section of Castleman's Corkscrew between Broadstone and Hamworthy Junction saw little use. For many years the line had only local importance, except on summer Saturdays when some Weymouth expresses used it. The line is still in use from Southampton to Lymington Junction in Hampshire, and from Hamworthy Junction to Dorchester.

Hamworthy branch

Passenger service withdrawn   1 July 1896
Distance   1.5 miles
Company   Southampton & Dorchester Railway

Stations closed   Date
Hamworthy *   1 July 1896

The station building at Hamworthy. The original station buildings are just to the left of centre.

This line was opened as a branch of the Southampton & Dorchester Railway to serve Poole, but it lay opposite the town and was reached by a toll bridge. Passengers to Bournemouth, which was five miles away, had to take a horse bus until Bournemouth got its first rail link in 1870. The line was doubled when the rest of the Southampton & Dorchester Railway was, but later singled when traffic was reduced. The line remains open for goods traffic.

* Known as Poole until December 1872.

Salisbury & Dorset Junction Railway *

Passenger service withdrawn	4 May 1964	*Stations closed*	*Date*
Distance	19 miles	Daggons Road **	4 May 1964
Company	Salisbury & Dorset Junction Railway	Verwood	4 May 1964

Daggons Road Station served Alderholt and Daggons.

* Closed stations on this line in Hampshire were Downton, Breamore and Fordingbridge.   ** Known as Alderholt until May 1876 and then Daggons Road until 1905.

Daggons Road Station in what is probably a pre-1914 view. The train appears to be headed by an Adams 4-4-0.

This line was authorised in 1861 and opened in December 1866 to link Salisbury with the Dorset coast. It was single track with passing loops at the four original intermediate stations (there was no station at Daggons Road until January 1876) and ran from Adderbury Junction, on the Salisbury to Romsey line, to West Moors on the Southampton & Dorchester Railway. It was worked by the LSWR from the outset and absorbed by that company in January 1883. During the 1920s there were six trains daily between Salisbury and Bournemouth, with one on Sundays.

Verwood Station.

Verwood Station

The staff of Verwood Station with a plate-laying gang.

Lyme Regis branch *

Passenger service withdrawn   29 November 1965   *Stations closed*   *Date*
Distance   6.8 miles   Lyme Regis   29 November 1965
Company   Axminster & Lyme Regis Light Railway

An early picture of Lyme Regis Station with a coach in the two-tone LSWR livery of salmon pink upper panels with 'invisible' green lower panels.

* The closed station on this line in Devon was Combpyne.

An Adams 4-4-2T, no. 30584, with a train from Axminster at Lyme Regis, August 1958.

There had been many early proposals for a railway to Lyme Regis but none of these became a reality. It was not until the Light Railway Act was passed in 1896 and a light railway order was granted in June 1899 that construction of this line began. The line opened in August 1903 and was worked by the LSWR from the beginning. The 12 ton axle weight limit, the steep gradients and the sharp curves on the line made the choice of suitable motive power difficult and Terrier 0-6-0Ts, specially purchased from the London, Brighton & South Coast Railway, and 02 tanks with water tanks only half filled were tried but only with moderate success. A solution was only found in 1913 when a decision was made to modify, with smaller water tanks, two Adams Radial tanks. This type had been introduced in 1882 and were already on the duplicate (or reserve) list, but they remained the line's mainstay until 2-6-2Ts took over in the early 1960s. The line was at a disadvantage with a terminus about half a mile outside Lyme Regis and 250 feet above it. It became part of the LSWR in 1907.

No. 30584 running round its train at Lyme Regis, August 1960.

Swanage branch

Passenger service withdrawn	3 January 1972	*Stations closed*	*Date*
Distance	10.1 miles	Corfe Castle	3 January 1972
Company	Swanage railway	Swanage	3 January 1972

Corfe Castle Station, the only intermediate station on the line.

Two M7 0-4-4Ts, nos. 30254 and 30667, at Swanage Station on 14 June 1963.

The station at Wareham, on the Southampton & Dorchester Railway, was some way outside the town as its citizens did not want the railway in Wareham itself. Attempts were made to promote a branch line to the Isle of Purbeck, which is in fact a peninsula, either to Swanage or the extensive clay workings, but there was considerable hostility to such proposals from Swanage itself. Eventually the Swanage Railway was promoted, but it had to alter its original plans to pass along the outside of the west wall of Wareham and forgo stations at Westport and Stoborough. Instead its trains had to travel over a mile along the Weymouth main line to Worgret, where there was no station, to a new junction there. The company obtained its Act of Parliament in July 1881 and opened in May 1885. It was worked by the LSWR from the start and was absorbed by that company in 1886. The line had through coaches to Waterloo and sometimes ten coach trains were worked through, while connections to Bradford, Manchester and Birmingham were provided by the Pines Express and the Somerset & Dorset Railway. Considerable amounts of clay were carried by the railway. The line was not among the lines proposed for closure under Beeching, but there were second thoughts and the passenger service was withdrawn with only the section from Worgret Junction to Furzebrook being retained for clay traffic. That was not the end, however, as a preservation group was formed and ex-Southern steam trains now run on it from Swanage to Norden, passing Corfe Castle.

Yeovil Junction – Yeovil Town

Passenger service withdrawn	3 October 1966	*Company*	Salisbury & Yeovil Railway
Distance	1.8 miles		

The town of Yeovil is in Somerset but Yeovil Junction Station is in Dorset while Yeovil Town and Pen Mill Stations were in Somerset. There was an intensive service between the Junction and Town stations to connect with most of the main line Southern services, and some services also ran between Yeovil Town and Pen Mill. The line opened when the Salisbury & Yeovil Railway opened in June 1860, but Yeovil Junction was built when the Yeovil to Exeter section opened. The Salisbury & Yeovil Railway became part of the LSWR in 1878.

Abbotsbury branch

Passenger service withdrawn	1 December 1952	*Stations closed*	*Date*
Distance	6.1 miles	Upwey *	1 December 1952
Company	Abbotsbury Railway	Coryates Halt	1 December 1952
		Portesham	1 December 1952
		Abbotsbury	1 December 1952

Upwey Station, January 1913. The picture is a reminder that before lined tankers were introduced, cities and towns were supplied with milk in churns carried by train.

* Known as Broadwey (Dorset) until January 1913. Between Upwey and Coryates Halt was Friar Waddon Milk Platform which was open between 1932 and 1939.

A 517 class 0-4-2T with a van and two autotrailers at Abbotsbury Station.

The first proposals for a railway to Abbotsbury were made in 1872 with hopes of developing stone quarries and iron ore deposits, although these never materialised. The Abbotsbury Railway was authorised as a standard gauge line in 1877. There were difficulties in the construction, first in raising the capital and then powers for a deviation had to be applied for to overcome the extortionate terms demanded by a land speculator. It opened in November 1885 from a junction with the GWR at Upwey and was worked by that company. After the local company went bankrupt it was absorbed by the GWR in July 1896. Passenger trains were worked through from Weymouth but the line was never profitable. Attempts were made to reduce the losses by the opening of the halt at Coryates in May 1906 and the introduction of steam railmotors (the line was later worked by 14xx class tanks and autotrailers). During the 1920s there were seven trains daily but none on Sundays. After nationalisation in 1948 the branch was transferred to the Southern Region.

A pre-1914 view of Abbotsbury Station.

ABBOTSBURY STATION

Bridport branch

Passenger service withdrawn	5 May 1975	*Stations closed*	*Date*
Distance	9.3 miles	Toller	5 May 1975
Company	Bridport Railway	Powerstock *	5 May 1975
		Bridport **	5 May 1975

Toller's station building is now at Littlehempston at the Totnes end of the South Devon Railway (Dart Valley branch).

* Known as Poorstock until 1860.

** Known as Bridport Bradpole Road between 1887 and 1902.

Bridport Station. The broad gauge has been slewed in to the standard gauge – note the gap between the running lines at the platform.

Bridport was to be on a number of planned main lines to the west, both broad and narrow gauge. The first of these was surveyed in 1843, but none of them materialised. The Bridport Railway opened as a broad gauge line from a junction with the GWR at Maiden Newton in November 1857 and was worked by that company from the beginning. The intermediate station at Toller was built cheaply in response to public pressure and opened in March 1862. The line was converted to narrow gauge in 1871 and the GWR took over the railway in 1901. When the line opened there were five departures from Bridport each day (but there was no Sunday service), although only the first of these, at 8.15 a.m., carried third class passengers. London passengers on this train could expect to arrive in Paddington at 4.55 p.m. The line was fairly busy in the 1920s with nine trains daily. Road competition led to the loss of goods traffic in 1965, but passenger services lingered on for another ten years.

Bridport Harbour extension

Passenger service withdrawn	22 September 1930	*Stations closed*	*Date*
Distance	2 miles	Bridport East Street	22 September 1930
Company	Bridport Railway	Bridport West Bay	22 September 1930

An up train headed by an 0-6-0ST at Bridport East Street Station.

A train headed by an 0-6-0ST waiting to depart from Bridport West Bay Station for Bridport and Maiden Newton.

The extension to Bridport Harbour opened in March 1884; the harbour was known as West Bay in an abortive attempt to encourage tourism. Bridport East Street was more convenient for Bridport town centre, but it closed to passengers in 1930. Freight services continued on the extension until 1962. The extension had earlier been closed between January 1916 and January 1920 and there were also periods of closure in 1921 and 1924.

Another view of Bridport West Bay Station with an 0-6-0ST and train having arrived from Maiden Newton.

West Bay Station

Weymouth & Portland Railway

Passenger service withdrawn	3 March 1952	*Stations closed*	*Date*
Distance	4.4 miles	Westham Halt	3 March 1952
Company	Weymouth & Portland Railway	Rodwell	3 March 1952
		Sandsfoot Castle Halt	3 March 1952
Stations closed	*Date*	Wyke Regis Halt	3 March 1952
Melcombe Regis	3 March 1952	Portland *	3 March 1952

An 0-6-0T, no. 2125, bridge testing with three other engines at Melcombe Regis, March 1909.

* This station opened in September 1902 and replaced an earlier station when the Easton & Church Hope Railway opened.

An LSWR train, headed by an 02 class 0-4-4T, crossing the Backwater on the old viaduct at Melcombe Regis.

This line opened on 16 October 1865 and was leased by the GWR and LSWR, an arrangement that continued until nationalisation. It was heavily engineered – there was a timber viaduct across the Backwater which was replaced with a steel structure in 1909 and, as well as that, after Westham Halt came the 700 yard long Marsh embankment, and after Wyke Regis Halt there was a 500 yard long timber viaduct across the East Fleet. The final part of the line to Portland was along the Chesil Beach. It was initially mixed gauge (broad and standard) but the broad gauge was only used for goods trains and those ceased from 1874. For many years after the line opened, trains from Portland to Weymouth had to reverse at Portland Junction and it was not until April 1909 that the station at Melcombe Regis opened alongside the terminus in Weymouth, but short of the junction. The halts at Westham and Wyke Regis opened the same year, prior to the introduction of an intensive railmotor service which at one time allowed Portland eighteen trains a day.

Rodwell Station.

A GWR train at Rodwell Station in 1909, after a loop was installed.

The train for Weymouth at Wyke Regis Halt.

WYKE REGIS HALT 18

J.CAMPBELL'S

A rail motor leaving Wyke Regis.

RAIL MOTER HALT WYKE REGIS 1909

The staff of Portland Station.

Easton & Church Hope Railway

Passenger service withdrawn	3 March 1952	*Station closed*	*Date*
Distance	3.5 miles	Easton	3 March 1952
Company	Easton & Church Hope Railway		

Despite the cramped layout at Easton Station there was an engine shed, seen on the right.

An ex-GWR 0-6-0 pannier tank, no. 3737, at
Easton Station with a railtour, August 1960.

This line was originally proposed in the 1860s but did not finally open for passengers until September 1902, having obtained further powers. It joined the Admiralty Breakwater Railway to complete the link into Portland and was worked by both the GWR and LSWR (later the Southern Railway). After 1931 it was worked solely by the Southern Railway. It had some steep gradients and was very scenic, running on a ledge between the cliff and the sea before turning inland. Hospital Halt was located near Portland and was only used by invalids, by special request, travelling to and from the Royal Naval Hospital. During the Second World War the line was closed from the end of 1940 until the beginning of 1945. Following the closure of the line to passengers, goods trains and specials for the Admiralty continued to run, and on one occasion an eleven coach train was hauled by two 14xx class tanks.

Easton Station.

Weymouth Quay Tramway

Passenger service withdrawn	1987	*Company*	Weymouth & Portland Railway
Distance	1.1 miles		

A saddle tank, no. 1337, 'Hook Norton', at Weymouth, *c.*1906. This 0-6-0ST was built by Manning Wardle and was formerly owned by the Hook Norton Ironstone Partnership in Oxfordshire. Note the bell for use on the tramway.

A GWR tank engine, no. 563, coaling at Weymouth Engine Shed, c.1906.

This line no longer sees regular traffic but occasional specials still run on it. The tramway runs almost entirely over public roads, which of course means that parked road vehicles have been a problem in more recent years. It opened in October 1865 and was worked by the GWR, although it remained the property of the Weymouth & Portland until nationalisation. Horse traction was used during broad gauge days which came to an end in 1874. After a demonstration Weymouth Council agreed to allow locomotives to be used and this began in June 1880. The line opened to passengers in July 1889, for Channel Island ferry traffic. For many years passengers had to use portable steps to get in and out of the coaches, but in 1933 the station was enlarged to two platforms. Traffic was heavy at times and in 1928 the GWR paid over £8,500 in harbour dues to the town council. Freight traffic was transferred to Southampton in 1972.

Weymouth Harbour. Channel Island ferries are in the background.

Somerset & Dorset Railway *

Passenger service withdrawn	7 March 1966
Distance:	26.8 miles (Templecombe [Somerset] to Wimborne Junction)
Company	Dorset Central Railway

Stations closed	*Date*
Stalbridge	7 March 1966
Sturminster Newton	7 March 1966

Stations closed	*Date*
Shillingstone **	7 March 1966
Stourpaine and Durweston Halt	17 September 1956
Blandford ***	7 March 1966
Charlton Marshall Halt	17 September 1956
Spetisbury ****	17 September 1956
Bailey Gate *****	7 March 1966

Stalbridge Station.

* The closed station on this line in Somerset was Henstridge.
** Also known as Shillingstone for Child Okeford and Okeford Fitzpain.
*** Renamed Blandford Forum on 21 September 1953.

*** Renamed Spetisbury Halt on 13 August 1934.
**** Known as Sturminster Marshall until 31 August 1863.

A Somerset & Dorset Joint Railway 4-4-0 crossing the River Stour near Sturminster Newton. This engine was built by the Midland Railway at Derby, although the picture was taken sometime after 1907 when it was re-fitted with a large Deeley boiler.

STURMINSTER NEWTON 12206

The Somerset & Dorset Railway was conceived as a coast to coast link to avoid the long and hazardous sea passage around Land's End. This was to be achieved by the amalgamation of two lines, the Dorset Central and the Somerset Central. The Dorset Central Railway had its origins in the stillborn South Midlands Union Railway which was planned to join the Midland Railway route to Bristol at Mangotsfield. The first section, from Wimborne to Blandford, opened in November 1860 and was, at first, worked by the LSWR. By the time the section on to Templecombe opened in August 1862 the Somerset & Dorset Railway had been formed.

The hoped for traffic levels were not realised and the Somerset & Dorset, in severe financial difficulties, sought its salvation in an extension to Bath where it could make a link with the Midland Railway. Although traffic increased it was insufficient to meet the line's obligations and, after an initial overture to the GWR, the line was jointly leased by the LSWR and the Midland in 1876. As these companies became part of the Southern and the LMS respectively in 1923, the Somerset & Dorset retained many distinctive features, including the royal blue livery which had first been adopted in 1886. However, the LMS took responsibility for the locomotives in 1930 and started to use its colours.

A member of the personnel of Shillingstone Station about to exchange the staff (which allows a train over a single line section) or else pass a message to the crew member on the footplate. The picture dates from 1898.

The Somerset & Dorset was a useful north–south link with a Bournemouth to Manchester Express and many long distance expresses to the Southern system at summer weekends, although these presented considerable operating problems over the single track sections. In 1958 the Western Region of British Railways took over control of the Somerset & Dorset and a long run down began. There was considerable bad feeling over the closure and the replacement express coach service took over 3½ hours to cover the 70 miles from Bath to Bournemouth; 70 years earlier steam trains had made the journey in just over two hours. Passenger services were withdrawn over the section from Corfe Mullen Junction to Wimborne Junction (three miles) in July 1920 and trains proceeded directly to Bournemouth instead.

A 4-4-0 and train entering Blandford Station.

Blandford Station

A 4-4-0, no. 16, at Blandford Station, *c.*1895. The locomotive was built in Derby in 1891.

A 4-4-0 at Blandford, 1898.

Blandford Station, August 1965.

Spetisbury Station. No 2.

Spetisbury Station. The stationmaster and a porter are on the platform while a permanent way gang are on the track.

Spetisbury Station. Again the disc and crossbar signal can be seen.

Bailey Gate Station, August 1965.

Somerset & Dorset Railway (Wimborne avoiding line: Corfe Mullen Junction – Broadstone Junction)

Passenger service withdrawn	7 March 1966	*Station closed*	*Date*
Distance	2.9 miles	Corfe Mullen Halt	19 September 1956
Company	LSWR		

As first built, Somerset & Dorset trains to the south coast had to reverse at Wimborne and it was not until December 1885 that this anomaly was removed and the majority of trains used the new line with only a few local trains using the Wimborne line up to 1920. The line was formally known as the Poole & Bournemouth Junction Railway and when it opened it ran parallel to the Wimborne line for almost two miles from Bailey Gate. This remained the arrangement until 1905 when the line was doubled to a junction at Corfe Mullen. Corfe Mullen Halt was opened in July 1928, the villagers having first asked for one in 1884.

Closed passenger stations on lines still open to passengers

GWR to Weymouth

Line/service	Date	Stations closed	Date
		Bradford Peverell and Stratton Halt	3 October 1966
Stations closed		Monkton and Came (Golf Links) Halt *	7 January 1957
Evershot	3 October 1966	Upwey **	19 April 1886
Cattistock Halt	3 October 1966	Upwey Wishing Well Halt	3 October 1966
Grimstone & Frampton	3 October 1966	Radipole Halt ***	2 January 1984

* Known as Came Bridge Halt until 1 October 1905.
** Replaced by Upwey Junction which was 805 metres to the south.

*** Renamed Radipole on 5 May 1969.